MASSACHUSETTS INSTITUTE OF TECHNOLOGY

Alfred P. Sloan School of Management

Center for Information Systems Research

VIRTUAL MACHINES
A CONCEPT THAT HAS COMPARATIVE ADVANTAGES
IN SECURITY, INTEGRITY, AND IN DECISION SUPPORT
SYSTEMS

by

J. J. Donovan and S. E. Madnick

REPORT CISR-24
Sloan WP 846-76

April 1976

MASSACHUSETTS INSTITUTE OF TECHNOLOGY

Alfred P Sloan School of Management

Center for Information Systems Research

VIRTUAL MACHINES
A CONCEPT THAT HAS COMPARATIVE ADVANTAGES
IN SECURITY, INTEGRITY, AND IN DECISION SUPPORT
SYSTEMS

by

J. J. Donovan and S E. Madnick

REPORT CISR- 24
Sloan WP 846-76

April 1976

ABSTRACT

This paper reconfirms the conclusions in our paper "Hierarchical Approach to Computer System Integrity," namely, that the virtual machine concept offers distinct comparative advantage for increased integrity and security in a computer system over other conventional approaches. Further, in this paper we describe our practical use of this concept in decision support systems.

INTRODUCTION

In our earlier paper [Donovan and Madnick, 1975] the authors showed that a hierarchically structured operating system, such as produced by a virtual machine system, should provide substantially better software security than a conventional two-level multiprogramming operating system approach As noted in that paper, the hierarchical structure and virtual machine concepts are quite controversial and, in fact, the paper has received a considerable amount of attention, such as in the paper by Chandersekarian and Shankar [Chandersekarian, 1976].

This paper provides a further confirmation, clarification, and elaboration upon concepts introduced in our earlier paper. Furthermore, based upon our recent research, it is shown that such virtual machine systems have a significant advantage in the development of advanced decision support systems.

Background and Terminology

In recent years there has been a significant amount of research and literature in the general areas of security and integrity As noted in our earlier paper, the reader is urged to use the references in that paper as a starting point for further information on these subjects. Of special note, the report by Scherf [Scherf, 1973] provides a comprehensive and annotated bibliography of over 1,000 articles, papers, books, and other bibliographies on these subjects   Other important sources include the six volumes of findings of the IBM Data Security Study [IBM, 1974] (the Scherf report is included in Volume 4).

Although there has been a considerable amount of attention and writing devoted to these areas, a precise and standardized vocabulary has not yet emerged. As stated in the recent paper by Saltzer and Schroeder [Saltzer, 1975]: "The words 'privacy', 'security', and 'protection' are frequently used in connection with information-storing systems. Not all authors use these terms in the same way." As an example of the lack of a comprehensive terminology source, Chandersekarian and Shankar found it necessary to draw upon six different references to define less than a dozen terms. Hopefully, as this area matures and stabilizes, it will be possible to reconcile these different viewpoints and arrive at a mutually agreed upon and standardized set of terminology. In the meantime, the reader may wish to study the glossary provided in reference [Saltzer, 1975], which by the way, indicates that protection and security are essentially interchangeable terms in agreement with our usage and in contrast to the opinions of Chander-sekarian and Shankar.

Hierarchical Approach to Computer System Integrity

In our earlier paper, it was shown that a hierarchically structured operating system can provide substantially better software security and integrity than a conventional two-level multiprogramming operating system. A virtual machine facility, such as VM/370 (IBM, 1972), makes it possible to convert a two-level conventional operating system into a three-level hierarchically structured operating system. Furthermore, by using independent redundant security mechanisms, a high degree of security is attainable.

The proofs previously presented support the intuitive argument that a hierarchical-structured redundant-security approach based upon independent mechanisms is better than a two-level mechanism or even a hierarchical one based on the same mechanism. More simply stated, if one stores his jewels in a safe, he may think his jewels are more secure if he stores that safe inside another safe. But the foolish man might (so he won't forget) use the same combination for both safes. If a burglar figures out how to open the first safe (either accidently or intentionally), he will find it easy to open the inside safe. However, if two different locking mechanisms and combinations are used, then the jewels are more secure as the burglar must break the mechanism of both safes. As explained in our earlier paper, the virtual machine approach can provide that additional security.

Clarification of Certain Points

The concept of "load" used in our paper is sometimes misunderstood, such as in reference [Chandersekarian, 1976]. It refers to "the number

of different requests issued, the variety of functions exercised, the frequency of requests, etc." [Donovan and Madnick, 1975, p 195], not merely the number of users. Hence, our conclusion is supported in that a complex operating system supporting a wide range of users and special-purpose functions is more likely to contain design and/or implementation flaws and thus susceptible to integrity failures than a simpler operating system. Others have also come to this conclusion. For example it is noted in the concluding remarks of the recent study of VM/370 integrity by Attanasio et al. [Attanasio, 1976] that "The virtual machine architecture embodied in VM/370 greatly simplifies an operating system in most areas and hence increases the probability of correct implementation and resistance to penetration."

There seems to be general agreement on the key point that there should be "...mechanisms that enforce the isolation of different layers" [Chandersekarian, 1976]. As previously stated [Donovan and Madnick, 1975, p 198], "in order to provide the needed isolation, future VMM's may be designed with increased redundant security..." A source of possible confusion may arise from the fact that some readers assume that our discussion of hierarchical operating systems and the VM/370 example are synonymous; whereas, the VM/370 example is exactly that: an example. Most of the VM/370 penetration problems, such as I/O, noted by Chandersekarian and Shankar [Chandersekarian, 1976] are attributable to the lack of independent redundant security mechanisms either in VM/370 or in the OS's running on the virtual machines. For example, under standard VM370, the CMS operating system provides minimal constraints on user-originated I/O programs This is usually viewed as one of CMS's advantages, from a flexibility point of view, but this does present unnecessary opportunities for penetration.

In the VM/370 integrity study by Attanasio et al [Attanasio, 1976], it was reported that "Almost every demonstrated flaw in the system was found to involve the input/output (I/O) in some manner." In other words, penetration was easiest in the area where the approach of independent redundant security mechanisms was not fully employed.

Flaws, such as noted above, need not exist in a hierarchically structured operating system Without elaborating unduly, Goldberg [Goldberg, 1972] has shown that it is possible to build economical hardware support for the hierarchical structure so as to eliminate the need for the VMM to be trapped in order to process operating system level interrupts In fact, IBM has adopted some of these approaches as part of the "VM assist" [Horton, 1973] hardware features.

Thus, although VM/370 provides an interesting and concrete basis for current-day hierarchically-structured systems, it was not originally designed with that purpose in mind and, correspondingly, contains some flaws These flaws are not inherent in the virtual machine approach and can be eliminated It is our understanding that various other computer manufacturers are also exploring this approach.

Additional Uses and Benefits of the Virtual Machine Approach

Our recent research in the development of advanced decision support systems, especially in the area of energy policymaking [M I T., 1975 and Donovan et al., 1975], has provided an example of additional uses and benefits of the virtual machine approach Advanced decision support systems [Gorry and Morton, 1971] are characterized by

- specifics of problem area are unknown

- problem keeps changing

- results are needed quickly

- results must be produced at low costs

- data needed for those results may have complex security

    requirements since they come from various sources.

This class of problems is exemplified by the public and private
decision-making systems we have developed in the energy area. We have
found that the problems that decision-makers in the energy area must
address have those properties.

A specific example of such a system can be found in our recently
developed New England Energy Management Information System (NEEMIS)
[Donovan and Keating, 1976]. This facility is presently being used by the
state energy offices in New England for assisting the region in energy
policymaking.

Many of the NEEMIS studies are concerned about the economic impact
of certain policies. For example, during a presentation of NEEMIS [Donovan
and Keating, 1976] at the November 7, 1975 New England Governors' Conference, Governor Noel of Rhode Island requested an analysis of the impact
on his state of a proposed decontrol program in light of likely OPEC oil
prices These results could be used in a discussion at a meeting with
President Ford later that afternoon. This situation illustrates several
of the requirements (e.g., results needed quickly and problem not known
long in advance) for an advanced decision support system.

In other studies, it is often necessary to analyze and understand long-term trends. For example, using data supplied by the Arthur D. Little Co. [Arthur D Little Co , 1975], we were able to trace the trends in total energy consumption in an average Massachusetts home from 1962 to 1974. We were interested in studying the amount of increased consumption, the pattern of increase over the years, and the extent to which conservation measures may have reduced consumption in recent years. Figure 1 is the graph produced by NEEMIS showing energy consumption versus time To our surprise, it indicated a roughly continuous _decrease_ in consumption for the average Massachusetts home throughout the entire period under study in spite of increased use of air conditioners and other electrical and energy-consuming appliances.

The object of this study suddenly changed to try to understand the underlying phenomenon and validate various hypotheses. In this process, it was necessary to analyze several other data series and and use additional models Several important factors were identified including·
(1) census data indicated that the average size of a home unit had been getting smaller, (2) weather data indicated that the region was having warmer winters, and (3) construction data indicated that the efficiency of heat generating equipment had been improving.

We had begun the analysis thinking that only consumption data was needed, as it developed, a sophisticated analysis using several other data series was actually needed This changing nature of the problem or perception of the problem is a typical characteristic in decision support systems. We have found similar problems in our work in the development of a system of leading energy indicators for FEA [M I T , 1975 and Donovan, 1976] and in medical decision support systems [Donovan et al , 1975]

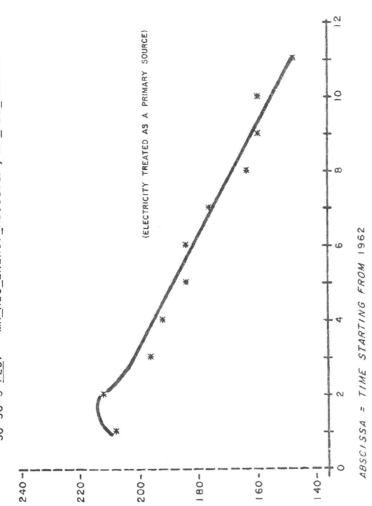

30 50 5 _PLOT_ 'MA_RES_ENERGY_ADJUSTED, MA_RES_ENERGY'

(ELECTRICITY TREATED AS A PRIMARY SOURCE)

ABSCISSA = TIME STARTING FROM 1962

* = MA_RES_ENERGY

FIGURE I. RESIDENTIAL CONSUMPTION OF ENERGY IN MASSACHUSETTS

GMIS Approach

To respond to the needs for advanced decision support systems, we have focused on technologies that facilitate transferability of existing models and packages onto one integrated system even though these programs may normally run under "seemingly incompatible" operating systems. This allows an analyst to respond to a policymaker's request more generally and at less cost by building on existing work Different existing modelling facilities, econometric packages, simulation, statistical, data base management facilities can be integrated into such a facility, which has been named the Generalized Management Information System (GMIS) facility.

Further, because of the data management limitations of many of these existing tools (e.g., econometric modelling facilities), we have also focused on ways to enhance at low cost their data management capabilities Our experience with virtual machines, discussed in the next section, indicates it is a technology that has great benefit in all the above areas.

GMIS Configuration

Under an M I.T./IBM Joint Study Agreement we have developed the GMIS software facility [Donovan and Jacoby, 1975] to support a configuration of virtual machines. The present implementation operates on an IBM System/370 Model 158 at the IBM Cambridge Scientific Center.[1] The present

---

[1] Special recognition must go to Ray Fessell of the IBM Cambridge Scientific Center for his assistance with the implementation and to Stuart Greenberg and Richard MacKinnon of the IBM Cambridge Scientific Center for their support of the entire Joint Study.

configuration is depicted in Figure 2 where each box denotes a separate
virtual machine. Those virtual machines across the top of the figure each
contain their own operating system and execute programs that provide
specific capabilities, whether they be analytical facilities, existing
models, or data base systems. All these programs can access data managed
by the general data management facility running on the VM (1) virtual
machine depicted in the center of the page.

A sample use of the GMIS architecture might proceed as follows.
A user activates a model, say in the APL/EPLAN machine (EPLAN [Schober,
1975] is an econometric modelling package). That model requests data
from the general data base machine (called the Transaction Virtual
Machine, or TVM), which responds by passing back the requested data.
Note that all the analytical facilities and data base facilities may be
incompatible with each other, in that they may run under different
operating systems. The communications facility between virtual machines
in GMIS is described in [Donovan and Jacoby, 1975 and Gutentag, 1975].

GMIS software has been designed using a hierarchical approach [Madnick,
1969, Madnick and Donovan, 1974, and Gutentag, 1975]. Several levels of
software exist, where each level only calls the level below it. Each
higher level contains increasingly more general functions and requires less
user sophistication for use.

Users of each virtual machine have the increased protection mechanism
discussed in our first paper [Donovan and Madnick 1975]. We have also
found increased effectiveness in using systems that were previously batch-
oriented but can be interactive under VM.

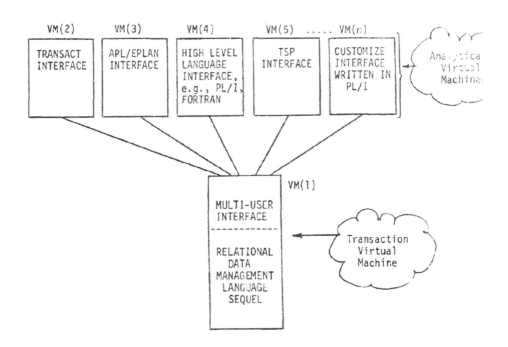

Figure 2:   Overview of the Software Architecture of GMIS

Conclusion

We remain enthusiastic about the potential of virtual machine concepts and strongly recommend this approach. VM technology coupled with other technologies, namely, hierarchical and interactive data base systems have distinct comparative advantages for a broad class of problems, especially in decision support systems.

We suspect that we have only scratched the surface of realizing the potential of VM concepts. One such area is to extend the configuration of Figure 2 to add access to other data management systems. However, more research is needed in the unresolved issues of locking, synchronization, and communication between the virtual machines and related performance issues.

We suspect our arguments will not completely resolve the controversy regarding virtual machine systems. But for users, decision makers, and managers, we want to add hope that this technology can greatly aid in providing tools to them.

ACKNOWLEDGEMENT

We wish to acknowledge the following organizations for their support of work reported in this paper.

The initial research on security and integrity issues were supported in part by the IBM Data Security Study.

The recent applications of the virtual machine approach to decision support systems have been supported in part by the M.I.T /IBM Joint Study on information systems. Special recognition is given to the staff of the IBM Cambridge Scientific Center for their help in implementing these ideas and to Dr Richard MacKinnon, head of that Center, as well as Dr Stuart Greenberg, coordinators of the Joint Study for their managerial support.

We acknowledge the members of the IBM San Jose Research Center for the use of their relational data base system, SEQUEL, and for their assistance in adapting that system for use within GMIS and energy applications.

The development of the New England Energy Management Information System was supported in part by the New England Regional Commission under Contract No. 1053068.

Other applications of this work were supported by the Federal Energy Office Contract No. 14-01-001-2040 and The National Foundation/March of Dimes contract to the Tufts New England Medical Center.

We acknowledge the contributions of our colleagues within the Sloan School's Center for Information Systems Research and within the M I.T Energy Laboratory for their helpful suggestions, especially those of Michael Scott Morton, Henry Jacoby, and David Wood

REFERENCES

1. Arthur D. Little, Inc.· "Historical Data on New England Energy
    Requirements" (prepared for the New England Regional Commission),
    Cambridge, Mass , September 1975

2. Attanasio, C R , P. W. Markstein, and R. J Phillips   "Penetrating
    an Operating System: A Study of VM/370 Integrity," IBM Systems
    Journal, No. 1, pp. 102-116, 1976.

3. Chamberlain, D. D. and R F Boyce   "SEQUEL   A Structured English
    Query Language," Proceedings of 1974 ACM/SIGFIDET Workshop, 1974

4. Chandersekarian, C. S. and K. S. Shankar: "On Virtual Machine
    Integrity," IBM Systems Journal.

5. Donovan, J. J., L. M Gutentag, D. Bergsma, and S. Gellis· "An
    Application of Current Systems Implementation Technologies to
    a Genetic/Birth Defects Information System," M.I.T. Sloan
    School of Management Working Paper, February 1976.

6. Donovan, J. J. and H. D. Jacoby. "GMIS   An Experimental System
    for Data Management and Anlaysis," M.I.T. Energy Laboratory
    Working Paper No. MIT-EL-75-011WP, September 1975.

7. Donovan, J. J. and H. D. Jacoby   "Use of Virtual Machines in
    Information Systems," M.I.T. Energy Laboratory Working Paper,
    March 1976.

8. Donovan, J. J. and W. R. Keating   "NEEMIS: Text of Governors
    Presentation." M.I.T. Energy Laboratory Working Paper No.
    MIT-EL-76-002WP, February 1976.

9. Donovan, J. J. and S. E. Madnick   "Hierarchical Approach to
    Computer System Integrity," IBM Systems Journal, No. 2, pp. 188-202,
    1975.

10. Donovan, J. J., L. M Gutentag, S. E. Madnick, and G N Smith
    "An Application of a Generalized Management Information System
    to Energy Policy and Decision Making -- The User's View,
    Proceedings 1975 AFIPS National Computer Conference, May 1975

11. Goldberg, R. P.: "Architectural Principles for Virtual Computer Systems
    Ph.D. Dissertation, Harvard University, Cambridge, Mass , November
    1972.

12. Gorry, G. A. and M. S. Scott Morton: "A Framework for Management
    Information Systems," Sloan Management Reivew, vol. 13, no. 1,
    Fall 1971.

13. Gutentaq, L. M.· "GMIS: Generalized Management Information System -- an Implementation Description," M S Thesis, M I.T Sloan School of Management, 1975.

14. Horton, F R.: "Virtual Machine ASsist Performance," _Guide 37_, Boston, Mass., 1973.

15. IBM· _Data Security and Data Processing_, Volumes 1 - 6, Form Nos G320-1370 - Ge20-1376, 1974.

16. IBM. _IBM Virtual Machine Facility/370· Introduction_, Form No GC20-1800, July 1972.

17. Madnick, S. E : "INFOPLEX -- Hierarchical Decomposition of a Large Information Management System Using a Microprocessor Complex," _Proceedings of 1975 AFIPS National Computer Conference_, 1975.

18. Madnick, S. E and J. J. Donovan: _Operating Systems_, McGraw-Hill, Inc., New York, 1974.

19 Madnick, S. E. and J. W. Aslop. "A Modular Approach to File System Design," _AFIPS Conference Proceedings_, Spring Joint Computer Conference, 34, pp 1-14, 1969

20. M.I T. Energy Laboratory: "Energy Indicators," Final Working Paper submitted to the F.E.A. in connection with a study of Information Systems to Provide Leading Indicators of Energy Sufficiency, Working Paper No. MIT-EL-75-004WP, June 1975.

21. Saltzer, J. H. and M. D. Schroeder: "The Protection of Information in Computer Systems," _Proceedings of the IEEE_, vol 63, no 9, pp. 1278-1308, September 1975.

22. Scherf, J.: _Data Security. A Comprehensive and Annotated Bibliography_, Master's Thesis, Massachusetts Institute of Technology, Alfred P. Sloan School of Management, Cambridge, Mass., 1973.

23. Schober, F : "EPLAN -- An APL-Based Language for Econometric Modelling and Forecasting," IBM Philadelphia Scientific Center, 1974.